ínspirations

PAPIER-MÂCHÉ

Over 20 creative projects for the home

ínspirations

PAPIER-MÂCHÉ

Over 20 creative projects for the home

MARION ELLIOT

PHOTOGRAPHY BY DAVID PARMITER

LORENZ BOOKS

NEW YORK • LONDON • SYDNEY • BATH

First published by Lorenz Books in 1997

Lorenz Books is an imprint of Anness Publishing Inc.
27 West 20th Street
New York, NY 10011

ISBN 1 85967 432 1

Publisher: Joanna Lorenz
Project Editor: Sarah Ainley
Photographer: David Parmiter
Step Photographer: Lucy Tizard
Designer: Ian Sandom
Illustrator: Madeleine David

Printed in Hong Kong

1 3 5 7 9 10 8 6 4 2

CONTENTS

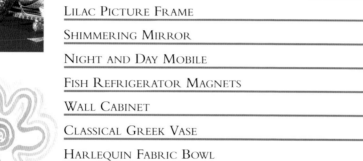

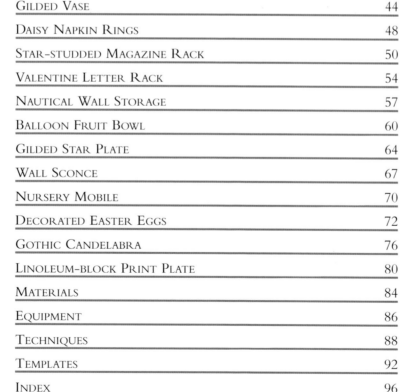

INTRODUCTION

The history of papier-mâché stretches across the centuries and continents. It is one of the simplest and most inexpensive craft techniques, and with imagination anything can be created, from delicate bowls to pieces of furniture.

As a child I can remember messing around with paper and glue. I have no memory of what I made but I bet I ended up with an uneven bowl created by plastering newspaper all over a balloon, the most exciting part being when I popped the balloon. Since then I have been constantly amazed by what can be made from papier-mâché. I love the tactile nature of bowls made from pulp; they look so solid, and then you pick them up and they are so light. It just makes me cherish them so much.

In this book we show you, with clear step-by-step photography, how to create 23 papier-mâché projects, from a practical magazine rack to a stylish candelabra. There is a comprehensive section on all of the basic materials and equipment you will need for the projects, plus useful techniques covering every method, with simple tips on tearing newspaper, making your own pulp, using molds and building your own armatures. Creating an object is one thing, but it is the surface decoration that will turn it into a unique piece for your home. We show you how to paint, gild, adorn with pebbles and even papier-mâché with fabric.

I hope this book inspires you to start collecting scraps of assorted papers and cardboard and to try out some of the stunning projects shown here.

PEBBLE WALL CLOCK

Natural materials on a papier-mâché base make an understated, stylish clock. A dozen sea-smoothed pebbles mark the hours: Their subtle shades and polished surfaces contrast beautifully with the textures of grainy recycled paper and rough natural twine.

YOU WILL NEED
pencil
compass
ruler
heavy corrugated cardboard
craft knife
cutting mat
white glue
newspaper
mixing bowl
paintbrush
fine sandpaper
white latex paint
decorative recycled paper
scissors
natural twine
clock movement and hands
strong clear glue
12 pebbles
picture-hanging eyelet

1 Draw a circle with a diameter of 10 inches on a piece of heavy corrugated cardboard. Cut it out using a craft knife and a cutting mat. Brush the circle with diluted white glue to seal it and let it dry.

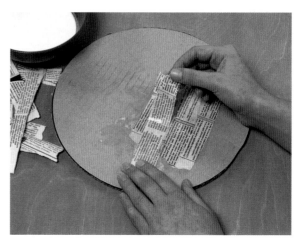

2 Tear newspaper into 1-inch-wide strips, coat them with diluted white glue and cover the cardboard with five layers of papier-mâché.

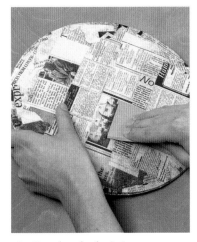

3 Let the clock sit in a warm place overnight. When it is completely dry, lightly smooth the surface of the clock using fine sandpaper.

4 Prime both sides of the clock with two coats of white latex paint, letting the paint dry between coats.

5 Draw a circle with a diameter of 7 inches on a sheet of decorative recycled paper, and cut it out. Use white glue to attach it to the center of the clock face.

6 Apply a thick coat of white glue from the outer edge of the clock to the edge of the paper circle. Starting next to the paper, coil the twine around the clock face until the whole area is covered.

7 Using a sharp pencil, make a hole in the center of the clock face for the spindle of the clock movement. Following the manufacturer's instructions, attach the movement and hands to the clock.

8 Turn the clock hands to 12 o'clock and make a mark on the twine border. Rotate the hands, marking the position of each hour on the dial.

9 Using strong, clear glue, attach a pebble at each mark on the twine to represent the hours. When the glue is thoroughly dry, attach a picture-hanging eyelet to the back of the clock.

TRINKET BOX

This useful little box glitters and sparkles with gold decoration, and there are small chunks of mirror embedded in the intricate handle on its lid. An armature made from cardboard provides the basic shape.

YOU WILL NEED
pencil
metal ruler
corrugated cardboard
craft knife
cutting mat
masking tape
white glue
medium and fine paintbrushes
4 marbles
newspaper
mixing bowl
epoxy resin glue
small mirror
hammer
chemical metal filler
matchstick
fine sandpaper
white acrylic gesso
gouache paints
paint-mixing container
matte and gloss polyurethane varnish
gold enamel paint

1 Draw and cut out the following shapes from corrugated cardboard: a 3¼-inch square for the base, four 2¼ x 3¼-inch sides, and a 4-inch square for the lid. Cut an 11 x ½-inch strip for the lip under the lid and fold it at 2¾-inch intervals into a square. To make the handle, draw a free-hand spiral shape with a ⅓-inch square tab for attaching the handle to the lid of the box.

2 Assemble the box and the lid using masking tape. Using a craft knife, cut a slot in the lid of the box into which to push the tab of the spiral shape. Seal the cardboard and tape with diluted white glue. Use masking tape to cover the four marbles, but do not attach them to the box yet.

▶

3 Tear a sheet of newspaper into 1-inch strips, then soak the strips in diluted white glue. Cover the box, lid and the four marbles in several layers of papier-mâché. Let the pieces sit in a warm place until they are completely dry.

4 Using epoxy resin glue, stick the marbles onto the box base as feet. Wrap a mirror in lots of newspaper and smash it with a hammer. Select pieces for the handle. Mix up the chemical metal filler, spread it onto the handle using a matchstick and embed the pieces of mirror. Let dry.

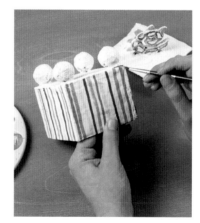

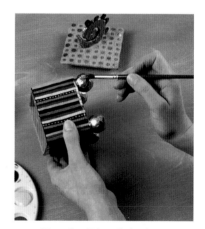

5 Lightly rub down the lid and box with fine sandpaper. Give them a coat of white glue, then prime with a coat of white acrylic gesso, remembering to paint over the filler around the mirror pieces.

6 When the base coat is dry, decorate the box and lid inside and out with gouache paints using a fine paintbrush.

7 Give the lid and the box several coats of polyurethane varnish, using matte and gloss for a varied finish. Finally, add gold details using gold enamel paint.

LILAC PICTURE FRAME

If you have a pretty picture languishing in an unattractive frame, use papier-mâché to transform it
into something stylish and original. Cut the basic shape from cardboard, then cover with
layers of papier-mâché before adding the decoration.

YOU WILL NEED

heavy corrugated cardboard
pencil
metal ruler
craft knife
cutting mat
wooden picture frame
masking tape
newspaper
wallpaper paste
mixing bowl
cotton balls
felt-tip marker
coarse string
all-purpose glue
white latex paint
2 paintbrushes
picture framer's wax gilt

1 Measure and cut out a piece of heavy corrugated cardboard $3\frac{1}{2}$ inches larger on all sides than the wooden picture frame. Cut out the central aperture using the wooden frame as a guide.

2 Lay the wooden frame on top of the cardboard one and tape it in place all around using the masking tape.

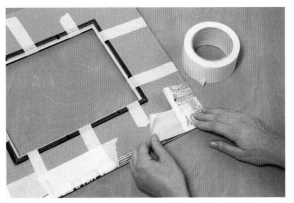

3 Fold a sheet of newspaper into a strip slightly wider than one side of the cardboard frame. Fold the excess under the frame and tape it in place. Tape the paper along the front of the frame. Repeat on the other sides.

4 When all four sides of the frame are lined with newspaper, tear some newspaper into 3-inch wide strips and soak them in wallpaper paste. Lay them over both edges of the frame until the whole thing is covered in papier-mâché. Let dry.

5 Cut the cotton balls in half using a craft knife. Using a felt-tip marker, draw a freehand guide around the frame for attaching the string and cotton balls.

6 Attach the string and cotton balls using all-purpose glue. Tear some newspaper into small pieces and soak in wallpaper paste. Paper over the string and cotton balls.

7 Paint the whole frame with two coats of white latex, letting the paint dry between coats. When the paint is thoroughly dry, gild the raised design using picture framer's wax gilt.

SHIMMERING MIRROR

In this variation, a small mirror is given lots of impact when it is set in a deep square frame painted in glowing blue and gold. Entwine a length of string around the outside of the frame for added interest.

YOU WILL NEED
double corrugated cardboard
pencil
metal ruler
craft knife
cutting mat
8-inch square mirror
white glue
paintbrush
weights
epoxy resin glue
newspaper
wallpaper paste
mixing bowl
coarse string
white latex paint
acrylic paints: cobalt blue, deep turquoise
paint-mixing container
sponge
rich gold gouache
gloss spray varnish
window scraper
2 picture-hanging eyelets
picture wire

1 On double corrugated cardboard, draw a 16-inch square for the back of the mirror, and for the frame draw four 16 x 4-inch strips and four 8 x 4-inch strips. Cut them out using a craft knife.

2 Place the mirror in the center of the square backing piece and build up the frame around it with a double layer of cardboard. Stick the cardboard in place using white glue. Place weights on top while the glue is drying.

3 Remove the mirror and seal the cardboard with a coat of diluted white glue. Stick the mirror in place using epoxy resin glue. Tear newspaper into strips and soak in wallpaper paste. Cover the front and back of the frame with four layers of papier-mâché, making a neat edge around the mirror. Let dry.

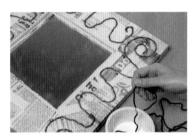

4 Seal the frame with a coat of diluted white glue. Dip the length of string in white glue and coil it around the frame. Glue a second length of string in the recess around the mirror. Let dry completely.

5 Cover the whole frame, including the string, with another layer of papier-mâché, using small strips of newspaper. Let dry thoroughly.

6 Paint the front and back of the frame with two coats of white latex paint, letting the paint dry between coats.

7 Paint the whole frame in cobalt blue acrylic paint, then sponge it lightly using deep turquoise. Let dry thoroughly.

8 Using a sponge, highlight the string pattern with rich gold gouache paint. Let dry.

9 Spray the whole frame with gloss varnish. Use as many coats as you like to build up a good finish.

10 Using a window scraper with a sharp blade, clean any paint and glue off the mirror.

11 On the back of the mirror, screw in two picture-hanging eyelets and string them together with picture wire.

NIGHT AND DAY MOBILE

Golden suns and moody blue moons contrast with one another in this attractive mobile.
Although mobiles are usually associated with children's rooms, this one is sophisticated
enough to hang up as a decoration in any room in the house.

YOU WILL NEED
corrugated cardboard
pencil
craft knife
newspaper
masking tape
wallpaper paste
small brass screw hooks
epoxy resin glue
white glue
medium paintbrush
white latex paint
paint-mixing container
gouache paints: blue, silver,
orange, red and white
fine paintbrush
gloss and matte varnishes
gold enamel paint
small jewelry jump rings
picture-hanging wire

1 Draw all the freehand shapes on the corrugated cardboard and cut
them out, using a sharp craft knife.

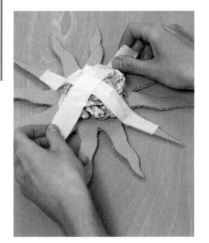

2 Tear some newspaper in to
pieces. Bulk out the shapes
by scrunching up the pieces of
newspaper, using masking tape
to secure the pieces in place.

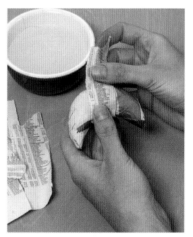

3 Cover the bulked-out
shapes in several layers
of newspaper strips soaked
in wallpaper paste. Allow the
shapes to dry overnight.

4 Screw in the brass hooks in the appropriate places for hanging the mobile. Use epoxy resin glue to secure the hooks to the mobile.

5 Coat the shapes with white glue and allow to dry. Then prime the shapes with a coat of white latex and leave again, until completely dry.

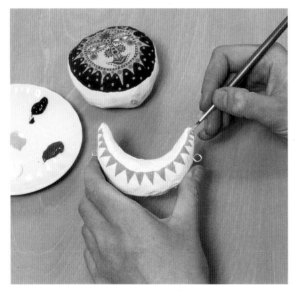

6 Mix the gouache paints to make a range of colors and decorate the shapes, using a fine paintbrush. Give each of the shapes several coats of gloss varnish, picking out some areas in matte varnish, to contrast. Allow to dry.

7 Add details in gold enamel, with a fine paintbrush. Assemble all the pieces, using the hooks and jump rings to join them together. Suspend the mobile from a length of picture wire, threaded through the hook and ring in the topmost shape.

FISH REFRIGERATOR MAGNETS

Make a school of colorful fish to swim across the door of your refrigerator. You can vary the thick-ness of the fish with the amount of papier-mâché pulp you use, but bear in mind that the more pulp applied, the longer it will take to dry.

YOU WILL NEED
pencil
stiff cardboard
scissors
papier-mâché pulp
newspaper
white glue
mixing bowl
fine sandpaper
white latex paint
paintbrush
water-soluble colored pencils
acrylic spray varnish
epoxy resin glue
flat magnets

1 Draw a selection of fish shapes on a piece of stiff cardboard and cut them out using scissors.

2 Press papier-mâché pulp, about ¹/₂ inch thick, onto the fronts of the fish shapes. Set in a warm place to dry completely.

3 Tear newspaper into 1-inch strips and soak in diluted white glue. Cover the fish on both sides with two layers of papier-mâché. Let dry. ▶

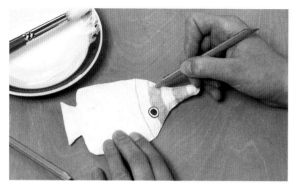

4 Lightly rub the fish down using fine sandpaper, then paint with two coats of white latex, letting the paint dry between coats. When dry, decorate the fish with water-soluble colored pencils.

5 Spray the fish on both sides with a coat of acrylic varnish. Let dry.

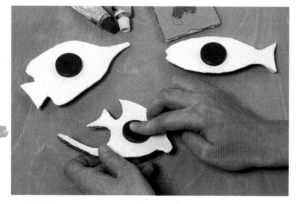

6 Using epoxy resin glue, stick a strong flat magnet to the back of each of the fish.

WALL CABINET

Layers of papier-mâché applied to strong corrugated cardboard make a substantial cabinet in which to display your little treasures. The terra-cotta tones used to paint the cabinet lend a strong earthiness, while the curly frame and glass "globs" strike a whimsical note.

YOU WILL NEED
pencil
metal ruler
double corrugated cardboard
craft knife
cutting mat
gummed paper tape
white glue
paintbrush
newspaper
wallpaper paste
mixing bowl
fine sandpaper
white latex paint
gouache paints: burnt orange, burnt sienna, dark blue, white
paint-mixing container
sponge
epoxy resin glue
glass "globs": 13 small and 6 large
acrylic spray varnish

1 Enlarge the templates at the back of the book and cut all the shapes out of double corrugated cardboard. Attach the sections of the long strip for the top using gummed paper tape.

2 Attach the base section to the arched back of the cabinet. Stick gummed paper tape all the way along the seam.

3 Add the pieces for the sides of the cabinet, with the cut-out sections to the front and toward the bottom of the cabinet.

4 Roll up the long strip for the top to bend the cardboard along the corrugations. Unroll the strip and tape it to the back and side pieces.

5 Place the frame over the front and tape in place all around the sides and along the base.

6 Insert the lower shelf and tape to the base of the cabinet. Tape the upper shelf in place 6 inches up from the lower shelf. Seal the cardboard with a coat of diluted white glue and let dry.

7 Tear newspaper into 1-inch strips and coat with wallpaper paste. Apply four layers of papier-mâché all over the cardboard and set in a warm place to dry completely.

8 Rub down lightly using fine sandpaper and prime the cabinet with a coat of white latex. Let dry, then paint the sides, frame and the edge of the shelf in burnt orange gouache. ▶

9 Using a small sponge and burnt sienna gouache, lightly sponge the frame and sides of the cabinet.

10 Mix blue and white gouache and paint the back and inner sides in pale blue. Using the blue paint undiluted, lightly sponge circles on the points of the frame.

11 Mix the epoxy resin according to the manufacturer's instructions and stick the glass "globs" onto the points of the frame, the extensions at the bottom, and across the front as shown.

12 Spray the whole cabinet with a coat of acrylic varnish and let dry completely.

CLASSICAL GREEK VASE

This stately vase demonstrates how papier-mâché can disguise and breathe new life into almost anything: it is based on a balloon and discarded yogurt containers. The final layer of natural-colored recycled paper gives the vase a stone-like quality, complemented by the twine decoration.

YOU WILL NEED
balloon
small bowl
newspaper
white glue
mixing bowl
heavy corrugated cardboard
craft knife
cutting mat
paintbrush
thick cotton cord
large and medium-sized yogurt containers
masking tape
scissors
pencil
strong clear glue
decorative recycled paper
fine sandpaper
natural twine

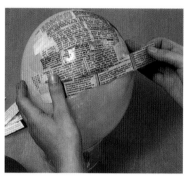

1 Blow up the balloon and rest it on a small bowl. Tear newspaper into 1-inch strips, coat the strips in diluted white glue and cover the balloon with five layers of papier-mâché. Set in a warm place to dry.

2 Copy the handle pattern from the back of the book and transfer it twice to the corrugated cardboard. Cut out the handles using a craft knife and a cutting mat. Brush diluted white glue over the handles to seal them and let dry completely.

3 Cover the handles with four layers of papier-mâché, working the strips neatly over the edges to keep the shapes sharply defined. Set them aside overnight in a warm place to dry.

4 Cut a length of cotton cord to fit around the top of each of the yogurt containers. Use masking tape to set the cord in place, to make a prominent lip on the neck and foot of the vase.

5 Using narrow strips of newspaper, apply five layers of papier-mâché to the yogurt containers and set them aside overnight in a warm place to dry.

6 Cut the bases out of the yogurt containers. Burst the balloon and pull it out of the papier-mâché. Position the larger container on top of the wider end of the balloon shape. Draw around the inside of the container and cut out the circle to make the vase opening.

7 Place the the narrow end of the balloon shape on the smaller yogurt container and glue and tape it in position. Attach the larger yogurt container to the top of the vase in the same way, then add the two handles.

8 Cover all the seams in the vase with three layers of papier-mâché. Set the vase aside overnight in a warm place to dry.

9 Tear the recycled paper into small strips and coat it in diluted white glue. Cover the vase completely with one layer of papier-mâché. Let dry.

10   When the vase is dry, smooth the surface slightly using fine sandpaper. Draw guidelines on the surface of the vase for the twine decoration.

11   Rest the vase on a small bowl. Paint undiluted white glue over each area to be decorated and apply lengths of natural twine, coiling them over the pencil guidelines.

HARLEQUIN FABRIC BOWL

For the final layer of this novel bowl, the technique of papier-mâché is applied to scraps of fabric, to give a glowing patchwork effect. Trim the edge of the bowl for a smoother finish, or leave it ragged for a more textured look.

YOU WILL NEED
bowl
plastic wrap
newspaper
white glue
mixing bowl
scissors
assorted fabric scraps

1 Use the underside of the bowl as a mold for the papier-mâché: Cover it with a piece of plastic wrap, smoothing it down well.

2 Tear newspaper into small squares and dampen them with water. Cover the bowl with one layer of overlapping strips.

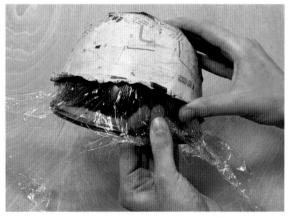

3 Soak some more newspaper squares in diluted white glue and cover the bowl with five layers of papier-mâché. Set the bowl aside in a warm place until completely dry.

4 Check that the papier-mâché is dry, then carefully remove it from the mold and gently peel off the plastic wrap. Trim away the uneven edges at the top of the bowl with scissors.

5 Make a selection of fabric scraps and cut them into small pieces in random shapes.

6 Dip the fabric scraps in the diluted white glue and cover the papier-mâché with them, overlapping them slightly. Begin on the outside of the bowl.

7 When the fabric on the outside of the bowl is quite dry, cover the inside in the same way. Let the scraps overlap the edge of the bowl.

8 Let the bowl dry thoroughly. The rim may either be trimmed with scissors or left as it is.

PEACOCK PENCIL POT

To make this useful pencil pot you could use a piece of the thick cardboard tubing that carpets or heavy fabrics are rolled up on. Make sure the layers of papier-mâché on the base are even and smooth if you would like your pot to stand upright!

YOU WILL NEED
hacksaw
wide cardboard tubing
stiff cardboard
scissors
white glue
newspaper
mixing bowl
fine sandpaper
white latex paint
paintbrush
water-soluble colored pencils
acrylic spray varnish

1 Using a hacksaw, cut a 4-inch section from wide cardboard tubing. Draw around the tube on a piece of stiff cardboard and cut out a circle to form the base of the pot.

2 Stick the base to the bottom of the tube using white glue. Tear newspaper into 1-inch strips and soak in diluted white glue. Cover the pot inside and out with two layers of papier-mâché. Set aside in a warm place to dry completely.

3 Rub down lightly with fine sandpaper, then paint the pot inside and out with two coats of white latex paint, letting the paint dry between coats. Decorate with water-soluble colored pencils.

4 When the decoration is complete, spray the pot inside and out with acrylic varnish to protect the design, and let it dry.

DECOUPAGE WASTEBASKET

Brown craft paper is used for the top layer of papier-mâché on this sturdy wastebasket and makes the perfect background for the gold gift-wrap decoupage decorations. Vary the size and pattern of the decorations to give depth and an interesting texture to the wastebasket.

YOU WILL NEED
compass
pencil
metal ruler
heavy corrugated cardboard
craft knife
cutting mat
gummed paper tape
sponge
white glue
paintbrush
paper
wallpaper paste
mixing bowl
brown craft paper
gift-wrap
acrylic spray varnish

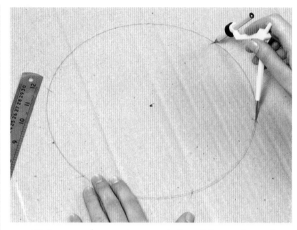

1 Using a compass draw a circle with a radius of 5 inches on heavy corrugated cardboard. Divide the circumference into 6 sections using the compass.

2 Reduce the radius of the compass $2^{1}/_{2}$ inches and mark off six intersecting arcs, so that the circle is divided into 12 parts. Join the marks to make a 12-sided shape and cut out using the craft knife.

3 Cut out a sheet of corrugated cardboard 30 x $13^{3}/_{4}$ inches. (The corrugations should run vertically down the sides of the wastebasket.) Divide it into 12 sections, $2^{1}/_{2}$ inches wide, and measure a line 2 inches from the top edge. Score along all the lines.

4 Fold over the 2-inch strip across the top to make the border of the wastebasket.

5 Cut 12 pieces of tape and stick them to each edge of the wastebasket base, moistening them with a damp sponge.

6 Turn the base over and use the tape to attach the sides to the base, bending the sides along the scored lines.

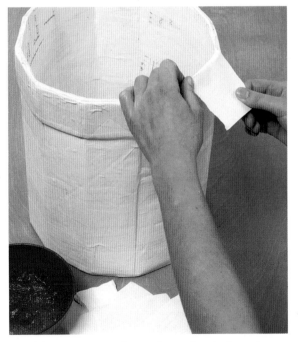

7 Use gummed paper tape to attach the side seam, taking the tape over the top edge and down inside the wastebasket. Seal the cardboard with a coat of diluted white glue.

8 Tear some paper into strips and soak the strips in wallpaper paste. Apply four layers of papier-mâché to the wastebasket, inside and out, and set in a warm place to dry.

9 Apply a final layer of papier-mâché using brown craft paper. Let dry. To decorate the wastebasket, tear images from a sheet of gift-wrap.

10 Paste the images with undiluted white glue and arrange them all over the wastebasket as you wish.

11 Tear some narrow strips of gift-wrap and stick them to the rim of the wastebasket and the line below the raised border.

12 Protect the wastebasket inside and out with a coat of acrylic spray varnish. Let dry.

GILDED VASE

Use a real vase as a mold for this splendid gilded container. Once you have achieved the basic form, you can add a rim and adapt the shape as you wish. If you put a glass jar inside the vase you will be able to use it to hold fresh flowers.

YOU WILL NEED
vase
petroleum jelly
newspaper
mixing bowl
white glue
craft knife
corrugated cardboard
jam jar (optional)
acrylic spray varnish
gummed paper tape
sponge
scissors
handmade paper
papier-mâché pulp
paintbrush
fine sandpaper
acrylic gesso
quick-drying size
Dutch metal leaf in gold or silver
large soft brush

1 Coat the vase lightly with petroleum jelly. Tear news-paper into 1-inch strips and soak them in water. Apply them to the vase in a single layer.

2 Dip more newspaper strips in diluted white glue and build up between five and ten layers of papier-mâché on the vase. Let dry thoroughly.

3 Using a craft knife, cut the sides and the base of the paper shape. Remove the vase.

4 Apply a layer of papier-mâché inside the halves of the vase to strengthen them.

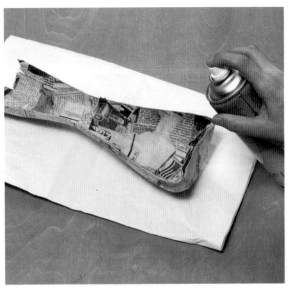

5 Cut a circular piece of corrugated cardboard to fit the inside base of the vase. Alternatively, find a jam jar that will fit inside the vase so that you can use it to hold water for flowers.

6 Varnish the vase all over, inside and out. (This is essential if the vase is to be used to hold water.)

7 Attach the two halves together with gummed paper tape. If you are not intending the vase to hold water, drop strips of paper soaked in diluted white glue inside to seal the seam.

8 Trim the top edge level using scissors. Make a rim from a circle of cardboard cut to fit the top of your vase. Tape it in place, then apply layers of papier-mâché over the top and edges. Let dry.

9 Soak some strips of handmade paper in diluted white glue and apply a layer all over the vase, to give extra strength, and smooth the surface.

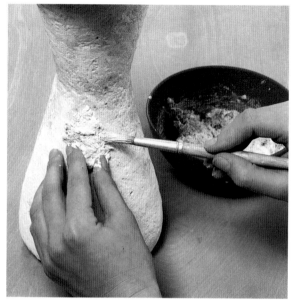

10 Apply a layer of papier-mâché pulp and set the vase in a warm place to dry completely.

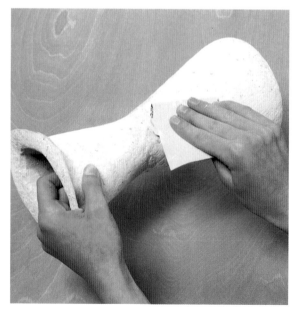

11 Smooth the surface with fine sandpaper, then apply a second layer of papier-mâché pulp and let dry again.

12 Paint the vase with two coats of acrylic gesso, letting it dry between coats. Give it a coat of quick-drying size, then apply Dutch metal leaf in gold or silver.

DAISY NAPKIN RINGS

The stiff cardboard tubes from rolls of fabric are an ideal size for making napkin rings, and a local store may be willing to give you some. If you use thinner cardboard tubing (from the inside of a toilet paper roll, for instance) you may need to apply more layers of papier-mâché.

YOU WILL NEED
hacksaw
cardboard tube
scissors
newspaper
white glue
mixing bowl
fine sandpaper
white latex paint
paintbrush
water-soluble colored pencils
gold marker
acrylic spray varnish

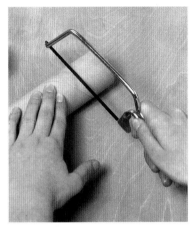

1 Using a hacksaw, cut a 2-inch section of tube for each napkin ring. Trim and tidy the edges using scissors.

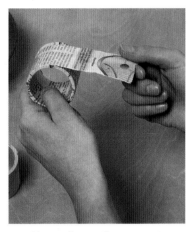

2 Tear a sheet of newspaper into narrow strips and soak in diluted white glue. Cover the rings inside and out with two layers of papier-mâché. Let dry.

3 Rub down lightly with fine sandpaper, then paint with two coats of white latex, letting the paint dry between coats. Decorate with water-soluble colored pencils, and edge with a gold marker.

4 Spray the napkin rings inside and out with a coat of acrylic varnish. Let dry.

STAR-STUDDED MAGAZINE RACK

Store your magazines and newspapers in this convenient rack, built from a frame of cardboard, covered with layers of papier-mâché and sponged and stenciled with silver paint against a deep blue background to resemble a starry sky.

YOU WILL NEED
pencil
metal ruler
double corrugated cardboard
craft knife
cutting mat
plate
gummed paper tape
sponge
white glue
paintbrushes
newspaper
wallpaper paste
mixing bowl
fine sandpaper
white latex paint
gouache paints: Prussian blue, pale gold and silver
paint-mixing container
stencil cardboard
acrylic spray varnish

1 Cut two rectangles from double corrugated cardboard, each measuring 16 x 12 inches. Draw a line 2 inches from one long edge of each piece, then divide this area into 2-inch sections. Using the edge of a plate, draw curves to attach alternate upper and lower points. Cut out.

2 To make the supports, cut out two rectangles 6 x 12 inches, and divide them into 2-inch sections. Using the edge of a plate, draw concave curves to attach the upper and lower points along each edge. Cut out.

3 For the ends, cut two equilateral triangles with 6-inch sides and four equilateral triangles with 2-inch sides. Place the two large-side pieces one on top of the other, and tape along the bottom edge with gummed paper tape.

4 Place one side support on top of the side piece, aligning the lower points with the bottom edge, and tape the upper points to the side. Repeat with the other support.

5 Insert the large triangles between the sides at each end and tape in place inside and out. Insert the four small triangles between the sides and the supports at each end and tape securely. Seal the cardboard with a coat of diluted white glue.

6 Tear newspaper into 1-inch strips and coat with wallpaper paste. Cover the whole magazine rack with four layers of papier-mâché. Use small pieces of paper to cover the edges and points neatly. Set aside in a warm place until completely dry.

7 Rub lightly with fine sandpaper, then prime the rack with a coat of white latex paint and let dry.

8 Using fairly dilute Prussian blue gouache, brush roughly over the whole surface and let dry.

▶

9 Using pale gold gouache paint, sponge a random design all over the rack.

10 Draw a small star motif freehand on a piece of stencil cardboard and cut it out using a craft knife. Sponge stars at random over the magazine rack using silver gouache paint.

11 Lightly sponge around the edges using silver gouache paint, then let dry completely.

12 Protect the surface of the magazine rack with a coat of acrylic spray varnish.

VALENTINE LETTER RACK

Ideal for love letters, this delicate and fanciful letter rack takes its basic shape from cardboard and galvanized wire. The letter rack is built up with layers of papier-mâché and is finally emblazoned with a bold, three-dimensional papier-mâché heart.

YOU WILL NEED
pencil
metal ruler
corrugated cardboard
craft knife
cutting mat
galvanized wire
wire cutters
round-nosed pliers
masking tape
newspaper
white glue
4 marbles
epoxy resin glue
fine sandpaper
white acrylic gesso
medium and fine paintbrushes
gouache paints
paint-mixing container
gloss polyurethane varnish
gold enamel paint

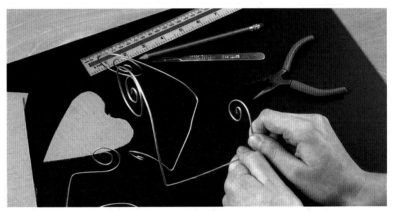

1 Cut two corrugated cardboard rectangles 8 x 3¹/₄ inches, and a heart shape 4¹/₄ inches high. Cut three lengths of galvanized wire 21¹/₂ inches long. Using round-nosed pliers, bend each of the wires into a large spiral at one end for the back of the rack and a smaller spiral for the front. Bend the spirals upward, leaving a flat area of 3¹/₄ inches in the center of each wire.

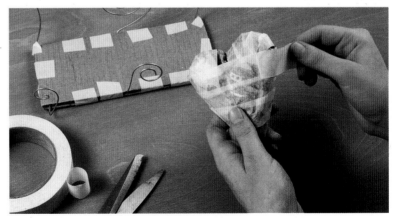

2 Sandwich the straight pieces of wire between the two rectangles of cardboard, securing everything using masking tape. Bulk out the front of the heart with scrunched-up newspaper held in place with tape, and tape the heart onto the center front spiral.

3 Tear newspaper into 1-inch strips and soak in diluted white glue. Cover the cardboard base and the heart with several layers of papier-mâché. Wrap masking tape around the marbles and cover in papier-mâché. Set everything aside in a warm place to dry. Attach the marbles to the base as feet using epoxy resin glue.

4 Lightly rub the papier-mâché with fine sandpaper, then coat it with white glue. Prime with a coat of white acrylic gesso, painting the wire and the feet as well as the base and the heart.

5 When the primer is completely dry, paint on the design using gouache paints.

6 Apply several coats of gloss polyurethane varnish, letting the varnish dry between coats, then add the gold detail to the heart and base and paint the wire and feet with gold enamel paint.

NAUTICAL WALL STORAGE

This jaunty wall-hanging provides safe storage for all those important little odds and ends that are always getting lost. Hung in the bathroom, it makes an ideal place to keep nail polish and cotton balls!

YOU WILL NEED
balloon
newspaper
wallpaper paste
mixing bowl
scissors
heavy corrugated cardboard
felt-tip marker
ruler
white glue
medium and fine paintbrushes
masking tape
fine sandpaper
white latex paint
picture-hanging eyelet
acrylic paints
paint-mixing container
acrylic spray varnish

1 Blow up the balloon fully to make a firm base for the papier-mâché. Tear newspaper into 1-inch strips and soak in wallpaper paste. Cover the lower two-thirds of the balloon with five layers of papier-mâché.

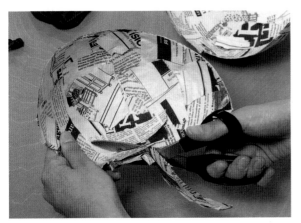

2 Set the papier-mâché aside in a warm place until completely dry. Burst the balloon and remove it. Using scissors, trim the top of the bowl evenly, then cut it in half.

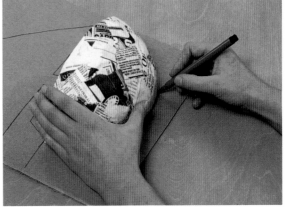

3 On a sheet of heavy corrugated cardboard, draw the mast, sails and cabin of the boat with a felt-tip marker and ruler. Place the half-bowl in position and draw around it to complete the boat. ▶

4 Cut the boat shape out of the cardboard using strong scissors. Seal the cardboard with a coat of diluted white glue and let dry.

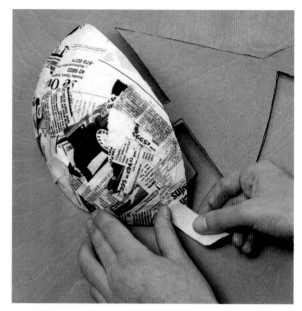

5 Using masking tape, attach the papier-mâché bowl section to the cardboard shape.

6 Cover the sails and the back of the boat with layers of papier-mâché and add another layer to the bowl. Set aside in a warm place to dry completely.

7 Rub lightly with fine sandpaper, then prime with two coats of white latex. Let dry. Attach an eyelet to the top of the mast. Decorate using acrylic paints and spray with varnish.

BALLOON FRUIT BOWL

A balloon makes a satisfying mold for a papier-mâché bowl. Remove the balloon when the papier-mâché is dry by popping it with a pair of scissors. An elegant foot made from a ring of cardboard gives this bowl a stable base.

YOU WILL NEED
balloon
newspaper
wallpaper paste
mixing bowl
scissors
stiff cardboard
pencil
ruler
masking tape
fine sandpaper
white latex paint
medium and fine paintbrushes
acrylic paints
paint-mixing container
acrylic spray varnish

1 Blow up the balloon fully to make a firm base for the papier-mâché. Tear newspaper into 1-inch strips and soak in wallpaper paste. Cover the balloon with five layers of papier-mâché, leaving the area around the knot bare.

2 Set the papier-mâché aside in a warm place until completely dry. Using scissors, burst the balloon and remove it. Trim the papier-mâché bowl to the desired height.

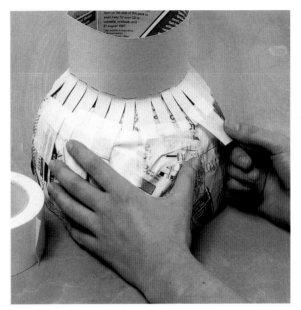

3 Cut a strip of cardboard about 5 inches wide and mark a line 2 inches from one long edge. Bend the strip into a ring and secure with masking tape. Cut ³/₄ inch inside the tabs all the way around up to the marked line.

4 Stand the bowl on its top edge and center the cardboard ring over it, bending the tabs outwards. Use masking tape to attach the foot to the bowl with all the tabs.

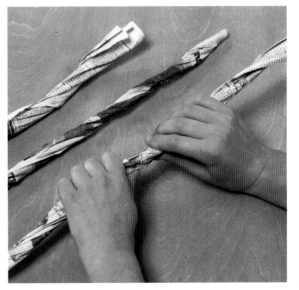

5 Cover the bowl and the foot in additional layers of papier-mâché and set aside in a warm place to dry completely.

6 Roll up some sheets of newspaper and twist them tightly to make ropes long enough to go around the rim and foot of the bowl.

7 Using masking tape, attach the newspaper twists to the top and bottom of the foot and to the rim of the bowl. Cover with more layers of papier-mâché and let dry.

8 Lightly rub with fine sandpaper, then prime with two coats of white latex paint. Let dry. Decorate the bowl inside and out with acrylic paints and finish with a coat of acrylic varnish. Let dry.

GILDED STAR PLATE

*A Renaissance head, delicately traced onto tissue paper with the lightest of pencil strokes,
forms the principal motif on this ethereal gilded plate. Surround the central image with
stenciled motifs and small squares of handmade paper for an intricate effect.*

YOU WILL NEED
petroleum jelly
dinner plate
newspaper
mixing bowl
white glue
thin cardboard
craft knife
metal ruler
cutting mat
scissors
gummed paper tape
sponge
paintbrush
papier-mâché pulp
fine sandpaper
acrylic gesso
picture for tracing
tracing paper
soft and hard pencils
tissue paper
stencil cardboard
gold paint
paint-mixing container
handmade paper
gold gift-wrap
acrylic varnish

1 Spread some petroleum jelly over the surface of a dinner plate. Tear newspaper into 1-inch strips and soak them in water. Cover the plate with one layer of papier-mâché. Soak some more newspaper strips in diluted white glue and apply a second layer.

2 Leave the plate in a warm place overnight to dry. Meanwhile, cut about 12 triangles out of thin cardboard. (Their size and number will depend on the circumference of the plate.)

3 Remove the papier-mâché plate from the mold and trim the edges. Use gummed paper tape on both the back and front to stick the triangles firmly around the plate, equally spaced.

4 Using a paintbrush, apply papier-mâché pulp to the front and back of the plate and the cardboard triangles. Set aside in a warm place until completely dry.

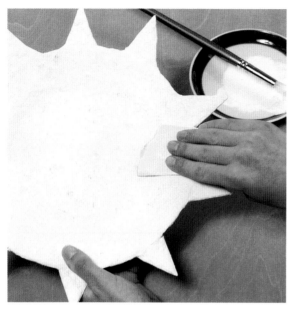

5 Smooth the plate using fine sandpaper. Apply a layer of acrylic gesso and let dry. Then sand the plate once again.

6 Make a tracing of a picture of your choice. Rub heavily over the back of the tracing with a soft pencil and transfer the drawing to tissue paper.

7 Draw a star motif on a piece of stencil cardboard and cut it out. Use a small sponge to make star prints in gold paint on small, roughly torn squares of handmade paper.

8 Cut 1-inch squares from a sheet of gold gift-wrap. Position the tracing, star stencils and gold squares on the plate and glue down. Varnish the whole plate and let dry.

WALL SCONCE

Delicate touches of gold glint in the candlelight on this pretty sconce. The printed pages used for the papier-mâché have been left showing as part of the decoration so, instead of newspaper, use a few pages from an old book for the final layer.

1 Enlarge the templates at the back of the book and draw them on a sheet of heavy corrugated cardboard. The back and base of the sconce are each made from three layers of cardboard for extra strength. Cut out with strong scissors.

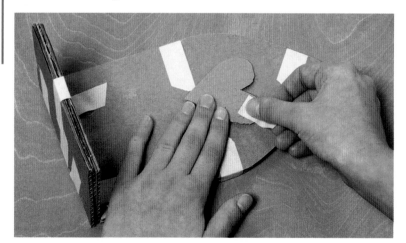

2 Using masking tape, stick the layers of the back and base together, and tape them at right angles to each other. Tape the heart shape to the upper back section, leaving room for the mirror. Seal the cardboard with a coat of diluted white glue.

3 Twist two lengths of galvanized wire together, then bend them into a curly S-shape to fit between the back and the base. Twist a second pair of wires to match exactly.

4 Tape the supports firmly to the back and base. Tear newspaper into 1-inch strips and soak in wallpaper paste. Cover the sconce with four layers of papier-mâché. Tear up a few pages from an old book and use for the final layer.

5 Set aside the sconce in a warm place to dry completely, then paint it all over with a wash of diluted white latex paint. When dry, color the heart gold and add an all-over pattern of spots, using a gold wax crayon.

6 Spray the sconce with acrylic varnish to protect the decoration. Apply a few coats to give a good finish.

7 Decorate the container of a night-light to match the sconce and glue it in the middle of the base. Glue a small mirror to the inside lower back of the sconce to reflect the flame.

NURSERY MOBILE

Children will love the primary colors of the sturdy shapes swinging from this mobile.
A length of bright red ribbon helps make this mobile a source of endless fascination
for young eyes.

YOU WILL NEED
coping saw
³/₄ inch pine batten
strong clear glue
pencil
heavy corrugated cardboard
scissors
11 screw eyelets
masking tape
white glue
paintbrush
newspaper
wallpaper paste
mixing bowl
fine sandpaper
white latex paint
acrylic paints
paint-mixing container
acrylic spray varnish
green garden twine and red ribbon

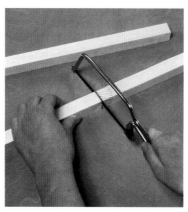

1 Using a coping saw, cut the wood into two 12-inch lengths to make the top of the mobile. Glue them together in the center, positioned at right angles to each other.

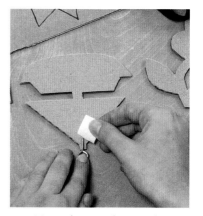

2 Trace the templates at the back of the book and draw the shapes on heavy corrugated cardboard. Cut them out and attach an eyelet to the top of each shape using masking tape. Seal the shapes with an all-over coat of diluted white glue.

3 Tear newspaper into 1-inch strips and soak in wallpaper paste. Cover each of the shapes neatly with several layers of papier-mâché. Set aside in a warm place to dry completely. Sand with fine sandpaper and prime with two coats of white latex.

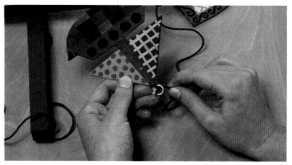

4 Decorate the mobile with acrylic paints and spray with acrylic varnish. Screw the remaining eyelets to the top of the hanger, under the center and the end of each arm. Use green garden twine to assemble the mobile and attach red ribbon for hanging.

DECORATED EASTER EGGS

These beautiful, glittering eggs make an opulent decoration at Easter. Use small strips of paper for the papier-mâché and sand it down well, to reproduce the faultless, smooth surface of a real egg. Decorated in different ways, the eggs will offset each other.

YOU WILL NEED

hard-cooked egg or egg-shaped mold
petroleum jelly
newspaper
white glue
mixing bowl
craft knife
12-inch gold cord
masking tape
fine sandpaper
acrylic gesso
medium and fine paintbrushes
plate
silver glitter
spoon
quick-drying size
Dutch metal leaf in gold
large soft brush
stencil cardboard
handmade paper
craft knife
cutting mat
gold and silver paint

1 Lightly grease either a real (hard-cooked) egg, or an egg mold, as used here, with petroleum jelly.

2 Tear newspaper into strips and coat with white glue. Cover the egg with papier-mâché and let dry in a warm place.

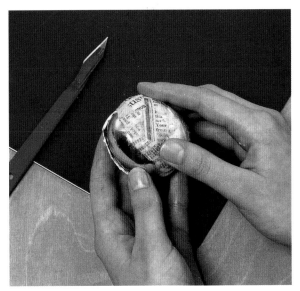

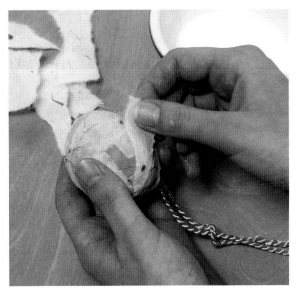

3 Using a craft knife, cut around the egg to divide the papier-mâché shell into two halves. Carefully remove them from the egg or mold.

4 Fold a 12-inch length of cord in half to make a hanging loop and knot the ends. Sandwich the knot between the two egg halves and tape together securely. Cover the entire egg with another layer of papier-mâché and let dry.

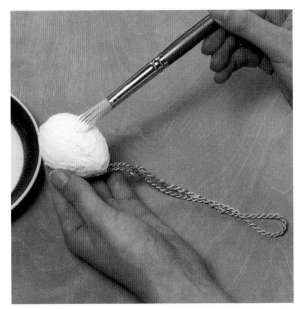

5 Smooth the surface of the egg with fine sandpaper, then apply a coat of acrylic gesso and let dry. Rub down lightly again.

6 Brush the egg with white glue. Put the egg on a plate and sprinkle it with silver glitter. Let dry.

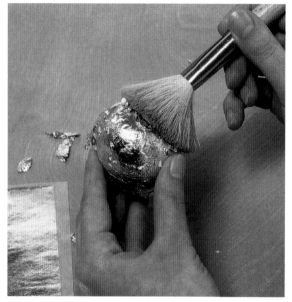

7 Alternatively, brush the egg all over with quick-drying size and, when tacky, apply Dutch metal leaf in gold, using a large soft brush.

8 For a decoupage egg, stencil small gold and silver motifs on handmade paper and cut them out. Paint the egg silver and stick on the paper decorations using white glue.

GOTHIC CANDELABRA

As if rooted in the base of this graceful candelabra, sinuous ivy entwines its stem and arms.
The basic structure consists of wire coat hangers and some cardboard, coated with several layers
of newspaper, and handmade paper to add weight and tensile strength.

YOU WILL NEED

pliers

3 wire coat hangers

jam jar

pencil

compass

ruler

heavy corrugated cardboard

craft knife

cutting mat

thin garden wire

gummed paper tape

sponge

thin cardboard

newspaper

white glue

mixing bowl

handmade paper

masking tape

papier-mâché pulp

paintbrushes

fine sandpaper

acrylic varnish

gouache paints in gold and silver

paint-mixing container

1 Using pliers, bend two wire coat hangers to make two curved arms for the candelabra. Bend the wire around a jam jar to get a smooth shape. Cut the hooks off the hangers.

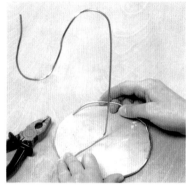

2 Draw a circle 6-inches in diameter on heavy corrugated cardboard and cut it out. Using pliers and a jam jar again, bend the lower end of each wire arm into a semicircle to fit around the edge of the cardboard and reinforce the base.

3 Assemble the structure, binding the two arms together with thin garden wire to make the stem. Attach the cardboard base to the wires with gummed paper tape.

4 To make the candle-holders, cut two 3¹⁄₂-inch circles of thin cardboard. Make a slit in the center of each and twist them into cone shapes. Secure with tape. Soak newspaper strips in diluted white glue and cover the cones with a layer of papier-mâché. Push them onto the ends of the wire arms and secure with tape.

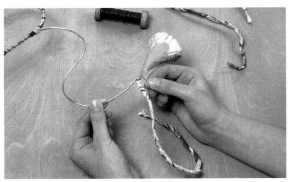

5 Twist long strips of newspaper and wrap them around the wire frame. Secure the twists with thin garden wire.

6 Soak strips of handmade paper in diluted white glue and cover the structure with a layer of papier-mâché.

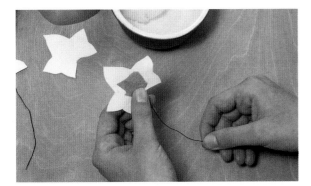

7 Bend a third wire coat hanger to make the stem of the ivy. Draw 8–10 ivy-leaf shapes on thin cardboard, cut out and tape each one to a short length of thin garden wire.

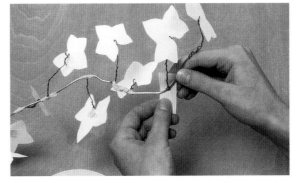

8 Use the thin wire stalks to attach the leaves to the ivy stem and secure with masking tape. Cover the ivy stem and stalks with handmade paper strips.

▶

9 Using thin garden wire, attach the ivy stem to the main frame. Twist the stem around the candelabra in an attractive shape and wire it in place.

10 Cover the whole candelabra in a layer of papier-mâché pulp. Let dry completely in a warm place.

11 Use fine sandpaper to smooth the papier-mâché, taking care not to disturb the shape of the candelabra.

12 Spray the candelabra with a coat of acrylic varnish to seal it. Decorate with gold and silver gouache paints and varnish again.

LINOLEUM-BLOCK PRINT PLATE

This beautiful papier-mâché plate takes its shape from the dinner plate used as a mold.
It is finished with hand-printed decoupage decoration, made from the linoleum-block printing
technique, and is finally embellished with some freehand painting.

YOU WILL NEED
white paper
felt-tip marker
tracing paper
hard and soft pencils
linoleum block
linoleum-block cutting tool
acrylic paints: sky blue, ultramarine
paint-mixing container
medium and fine paintbrushes
scissors
dinner plate
plastic wrap
newspaper
wallpaper paste
mixing bowl
fine sandpaper
white latex paint
glue stick
acrylic spray varnish

1 Work out the fish design on paper, using bold lines that will suit the linoleum-block cutting technique.

2 Trace the design and rub over the back of the tracing with a soft pencil. Transfer the drawing to a piece of linoleum block.

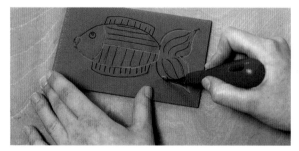

3 Using a linoleum-block cutting tool, cut out the lines of the fish design. Take care not to gouge too deeply into the linoleum block.

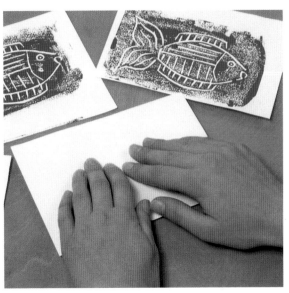

4 Cover the linoleum block with sky blue acrylic paint, using broad, light brushstrokes. Do not overload the brush or let the paint flood into the grooves of the design.

5 Lay a sheet of paper carefully over the design and press down evenly. Repeat to make as many prints as you need to decorate your plate.

6 When the paint is dry, cut out all the fish prints using scissors and reserve them while you make the plate.

7 Cover a dinner plate with plastic wrap. Tear newspaper into 1-inch strips and soak in wallpaper paste. Cover the plate with five layers of papier-mâché and set aside in a warm place until dry. ▶

8 Remove the papier-mâché carefully from the mold and peel away the plastic wrap. Trim the edges of the plate and finish them and the back neatly with another layer of papier-mâché.

9 When the plate is completely dry, smooth it with fine sandpaper and paint both sides with two coats of white latex. Let dry, then glue on the fish prints.

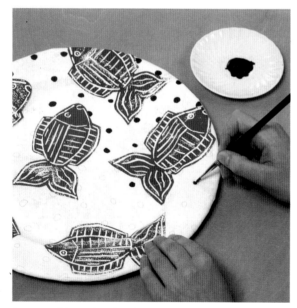

10 Using a fine brush and ultramarine acrylic paint, add a random pattern of spots all over the white areas of the plate.

11 Let the paint dry, then spray the plate on both sides with a protective coat of acrylic varnish and let dry.

MATERIALS

CORRUGATED CARDBOARD

Cardboard of "double wall" construction – with two rows of corrugations – makes a strong base for papier-mâché. It is especially good for making a permanent armature for large or complicated structures, as it remains inside the finished object, adding strength.

HOT GLUE GUN AND GLUE STICKS

Glue guns melt sticks of solid glue; the liquid glue is then squeezed through a nozzle at the end of the gun. Glue guns are ideal for holding together heavy sheets of cardboard as the glue dries very quickly to create a strong bond. Always follow the manufacturer's instructions when using a glue gun.

NEWSPAPER

Many papers can be used to make papier-mâché but the most pliable – and the most readily available – is newspaper. Newspaper comes in various weights and qualities: full-size newspapers are printed on finer paper than tabloids and are stronger and easier to handle when wet. Newspaper is available in a range of colors.

PAINTS

If decorating your papier-mâché with paints, apply two coats of non-toxic white paint as a primer, to seal the surface and hide the newspaper text. Use white latex, poster or powder paint as a primer if you intend to decorate with poster or gouache paints. If you wish to use acrylic paints for the decoration, use white acrylic paint or acrylic gesso as a primer. Acrylic paint is water-based. It dries to a plastic, waterproof finish and gives very good coverage. Acrylic paints come in a variety of finishes. Poster paint is also water-based. It is not waterproof when dry and will need sealing with varnish to become permanent. Poster paints come in a very wide range of colours.

POWDERED GLUE

Non-toxic powdered glue granules can be obtained at craft and hobby stores. The powder is mixed with water to a fairly stiff consistency. Powdered glue dries more slowly than white glue and makes the papier-mâché more soggy.

RECYCLED PAPER

There is now a wide range of exciting and beautiful recycled paper available that is good for adding a final, decorative surface to an item that is to be left unpainted. As these papers generally have no definite grain, they are often difficult to tear into long strips.

TISSUE PAPER

Colored tissue is very delicate and hard to handle when wet, and is simpler to use in conjunction with newspaper than on its own. However, beautifully translucent objects can be made by pressing gluey tissue paper into greased molds.

VARNISH

Varnish is used to seal the papier-mâché. If you use water-based paints such as poster, powder or gouache, use a polyurethane-based varnish. Only use varnish in well-ventilated conditions.

WHITE GLUE

White glue makes strong, quick-drying papier-mâché. Always use a children's non-toxic variety. The glue should be diluted with water to the consistency of light cream.

Clockwise from top center: newspaper, tissue paper, corrugated cardboard, powdered glue, white glue, varnish, hot glue gun and glue sticks, recycled papers, latex paint, poster paints, acrylic paints.

EQUIPMENT

BALLOONS

Balloons are great molds for making round objects such as vases and piggy banks. As with all molds, the surface of the balloon should be lightly greased with petroleum jelly before use so that the papier-mâché can be easily removed.

CRAFT KNIFE AND CUTTING MAT

These two items of equipment are very useful for cutting heavy materials such as corrugated cardboard. Always use a metal ruler with a craft knife, as a plastic ruler will not withstand the pressure from the knife.

MASKING TAPE

This is a removable paper tape that is very useful for holding together heavy materials such as cardboard while glued seams dry or while papier-mâché is being applied.

MOLDS

All sorts of things can be used as simple molds for papier-mâché. Old, unwanted china plates, molds and dishes are ideal. Before the papier-mâché is applied, a thin layer of petroleum jelly should be used to grease the surface of the mold so that the paper may be removed once it has dried. When selecting a mold, choose one that has no undercuts; no part of the mold should be wider than the opening from which the papier-mâché is to be removed. If this golden rule is not observed, it will be impossible to remove the paper shell.

PAINTBRUSHES

Wide decorators' brushes are good for priming papier-mâché, as they cover a large surface area quickly. Buy the best quality that you can afford; very cheap brushes are not worth buying as they constantly shed hair, making it difficult to obtain a smooth finish. Fine sable, sable/nylon or nylon brushes are good for applying poster and gouache paints, while thicker brushes that will withstand more washing should be used with acrylic paints.

PETROLEUM JELLY

A thin layer of petroleum jelly should be used to lightly grease the surface of molds so that the dry papier-mâché shell can be easily removed.

PLASTICINE

Plasticine can be used as a mold to make three-dimensional shapes from papier-mâché. The surface of the plasticine should be lightly greased using petroleum jelly before the papier-mâché is applied, so that the paper shell can be easily removed.

SANDPAPER

A fine grade sandpaper is useful for rubbing down the surface of unprimed papier-mâché to remove lumps and bumps and provide a good, smooth painting surface. Always wear a protective face mask when rubbing down papier-mâché.

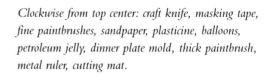

Clockwise from top center: craft knife, masking tape, fine paintbrushes, sandpaper, plasticine, balloons, petroleum jelly, dinner plate mold, thick paintbrush, metal ruler, cutting mat.

TECHNIQUES

Papier-mâché is a delightfully simple craft, and it is possible to learn the basic techniques very quickly. Once you have mastered a few simple skills, you will be able to tackle projects of some complexity with confidence, and with pleasing results.

USING A PLATE OR BOWL AS A MOLD

1 Coat the surface of the mold lightly using petroleum jelly, to ensure that the paper shape can be removed easily when dry.

2 Tear newspaper into strips approximately 1 inch wide and long enough to stretch across the mold. Coat each strip with diluted white glue (equal parts of glue and water) or wallpaper paste and place it in the mold.

3 When the first layer of paper strips is complete add the second, laying the strips at right angles to the previous layer. Add any additional layers in the same way.

USING A PLASTICINE SHAPE AS A MOLD

1 Form the plasticine into your desired shape. Lightly grease the plasticine using petroleum jelly. Using thin strips of newspaper, cover the shape with five layers of papier-mâché. Set it aside in a warm place to dry thoroughly.

2 Draw a cutting-line all the way around the edge of the shape. Using a craft knife, cut slowly and carefully around the shape to divide it in half. Gently pry the plasticine from each paper shell.

3 Fit the empty paper halves together, matching the cut edges exactly. Attach them using strips of masking tape, and cover the seam with three layers of papier-mâché using thin strips of newspaper.

1 When the surface of the paper in the mold is dry, gently pull back the edge and, if it seems almost dry underneath, insert a blunt knife and gently pry the paper away from the mold. Turn the paper shell upside down to dry completely.

2 Trim the raw edge from the paper shape using scissors, following the indent of the edge of the mold to ensure an accurate curve.

3 To prevent the layers of paper from coming apart, bind the edges of the paper shape using small, thin strips of newspaper.

MAKING A CARDBOARD ARMATURE

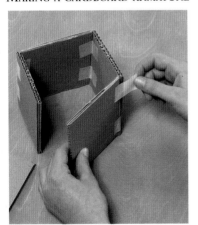

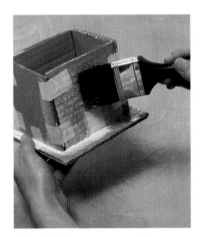

1 Cut the pieces for the armature from heavy corrugated cardboard. Tape the main structure together using masking tape.

2 Tape the main structure to the base of the armature.

3 Seal the armature with a coat of diluted white glue. This will prevent the cardboard from warping when papier-mâché is applied.

PREPARING THE SURFACE OF THE PAPIER-MÂCHÉ FOR PAINTING

The surface of the papier-mâché should be primed before painting to conceal the newsprint and to provide a good ground for decoration.

1 Gently smooth the surface of the papier-mâché, using fine sandpaper, before priming the surface with a coat of white latex.

2 Apply the first coat of white latex paint and let the object dry completely in a well-ventilated area.

3 Rub the dry paint lightly using fine sandpaper, and apply a second coat of paint. Once this has dried, the papier-mâché may be decorated.

PROTECTING YOUR HANDS

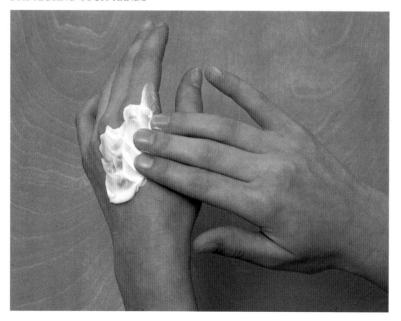

Although you should always use non-toxic, fungicide-free glues and pastes, more protection may be needed if you have sensitive skin. A layer of barrier cream rubbed into the hands before you start will help prevent problems, but if you suffer any discomfort when using the various glues, wear a pair of surgeon's thin rubber gloves to protect your skin. It is a good idea to rub rich moisturizer into your hands before you begin, as it makes washing off the glue much easier, particularly if you are using white glue.

TEARING NEWSPAPER

Sheets of newsprint have a definite grain, usually running from the top to the bottom of the newspaper.

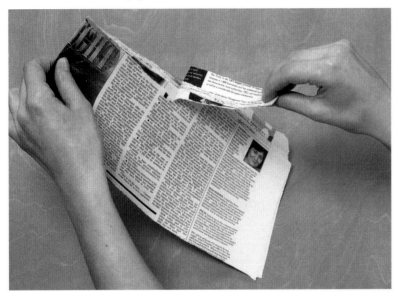

1 If you try to tear a sheet of newspaper against the grain – from side to side – it is impossible to control.

2 If newspaper is torn along the grain it is possible to produce very regular strips, as wide or narrow as you need.

PAPIER-MÂCHÉ PULP

You can buy prepared papier-mâché pulp, but it is easy to make at home. Use it for molded projects such as bowls and for building up sculpted shapes: just push it into shape with your hands or a stiff paintbrush. Allow plenty of time for drying, which may take several days.

YOU WILL NEED
5 sheets newspaper
saucepan
spoon
blender
plastic box
5 teaspoons white glue
2 teaspoons wallpaper paste
1 teaspoon plaster of Paris
1 teaspoon linseed oil

1 Tear the paper into pieces about 1-inch square and put them in an old saucepan with water to cover. Simmer for about 30 minutes.

2 Spoon the paper and any remaining water into a blender and blend to a pulp. Pour into a suitable container. (Lidded plastic boxes are ideal, because the pulp keeps for several weeks.)

3 Add the white glue, wallpaper paste, plaster of Paris and linseed oil. Stir vigorously, and the pulp is ready to use.

TEMPLATES

Wall Sconce
PP. 67–69

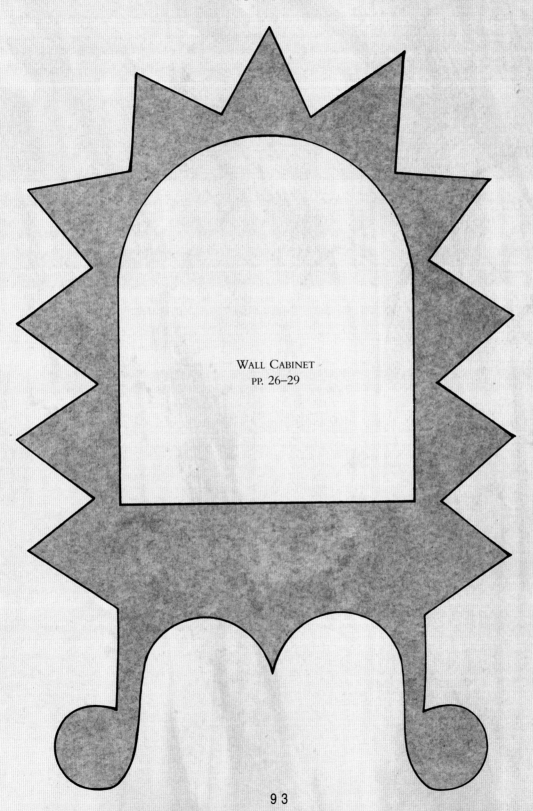

WALL CABINET
PP. 26–29

NURSERY MOBILE
PP. 70–1

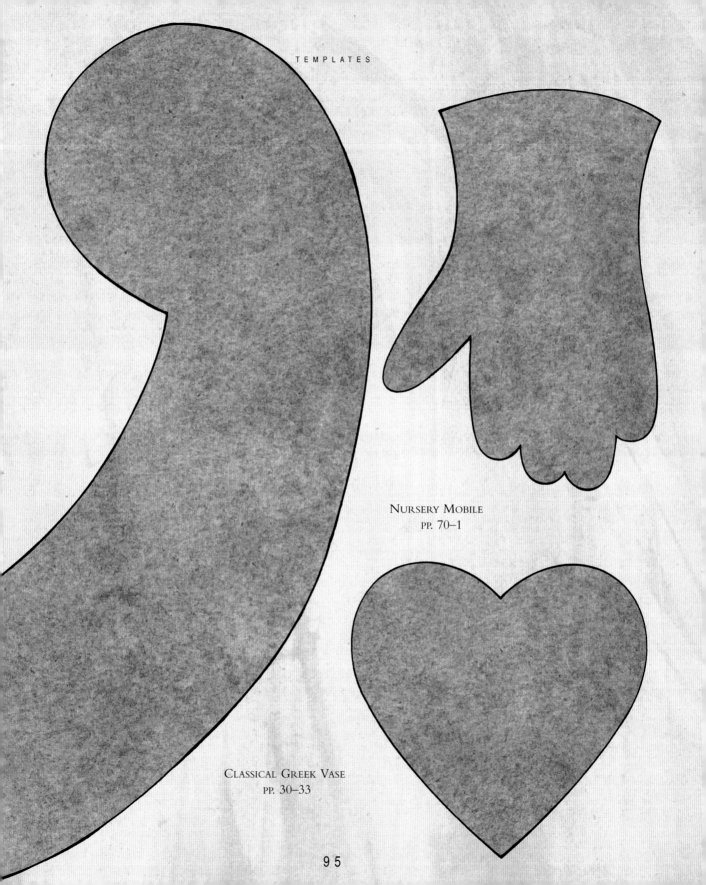

NURSERY MOBILE
PP. 70–1

CLASSICAL GREEK VASE
PP. 30–33

INDEX

The Publishers would like to thank the following artists for the beautiful projects photographed in this book:
Madeleine Adams: Fish Refrigerator Magnets, Peacock Pencil Pot, Daisy Napkin Rings; Petra Boase: Harlequin Fabric Bowl;
Gerry Copp: Shimmering Mirror, Wall Cabinet, Decoupage Wastebasket, Star-studded Magazine Rack; Ken Eardley:
Boat Wall Storage, Balloon Fruit Bowl, Wall Sconce, Nursery Mobile, Linoleum-block Print Plate; Marion Elliot: Pebble Wall
Clock, Classical Greek Vase; Emma Hardy: Lilac Picture Frame; Kim Rowley: Night and Day Mobile, Trinket Box,
Valentine Letter Rack; Kerry Skinner: Gilded Vase, Gilded Star Plate, Decorated Easter Eggs, Gothic Candelabra.